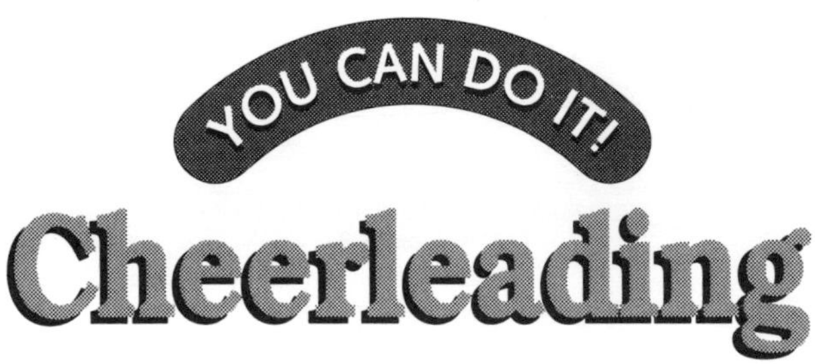

BY CINDY DANIELSON

1227 West Magnolia
Suite 500
Fort Worth, Texas 76104

Published 1993.
ISBN 1-56530-005-X

Printed in the United States of America.

10 9 8 7 6 5 4 3 2

Cover Illustration by Gregg Valley
Design by Cheryl Corbitt
Special thanks to the cheerleaders
of Arlington Heights High School in Fort Worth, Texas

YOU CAN DO IT!

Cheerleading

Contents

YOU CAN DO IT!

1 A History of Cheerleading

What is cheerleading and how did it develop into the sport that it is today? According to cheerleading historian Randall Neil, cheerleading began one day in early November of 1898. A student at the University of Minnesota stood up at a football game and encouraged the other fans to join in a cheer he had made up. That was all it took. Soon, colleges and universities began assigning "yellmen" to lead sideline chants at football and basketball games. They were called "yellmen" because it wasn't until later — in the 1920s — that women joined in the fun. The decade of the 1940s saw an even greater interest in cheerleading activities. Teams of cheerleaders, representing their individual schools, had long since decided it would look better for them to wear outfits that coordinated with their schools' colors. The idea of wearing matching uniforms created a special need for cheerleaders everywhere. They needed a special store where equipment and uniforms could be purchased.

A man by the name of Lawrence Herkimer, from Dallas, Texas, was the first to recognize that need. He formed the first cheerleading company. He became known as a pioneer in the field of cheerleading. In fact, he was given a very special honor for his contribution to the sport. One of cheerleading's finest jumps, called "the Herkie," was named after Herkimer. And today, some 50 years later, his company is still in business!

Cheerleading has become a popular sport nationwide and cheerleaders, or yell leaders as they are sometimes called, are an exciting part of the action. It's not just football and

The "Herkie" was created by Lawrence Herkimer more than 50 years ago and is still a popular jump.

basketball! In the 1990s, it is also volleyball, soccer, rugby, track and field . . . and much more.

Give Me a 'C' for Communicate!

Know the Cheers

A cheerleader is a communicator — a person who gives information. This means it is important that a cheerleader know the cheers. Think what would happen if he or she stood up in front of the fans and couldn't remember the cheer. How embarrassing!

Therefore, it is one of a cheerleader's first responsibilities — know your cheers.

HINT: Write the words on a piece of paper and tape it to the inside of your megaphone!

Know the Sports

Another important responsibility of the cheerleader is to know about the different games at which he or she cheers. You would not want to lead the fans in a victory yell if it were the other team that had just scored the go-ahead touchdown.

If you're having trouble learning about a particular sport, ask a favorite coach or player of that sport to give you a few pointers. They will be able to answer any questions you might have.

Get the Fans Involved

The true test of a cheerleader is not how many yells he or she remembers. The true test is being able to get the fans to join in the cheering.

One popular way to keep your team's fans interested is to choose yells that ask questions that they must answer. Many sideline chants have a simple "echo" for the crowd to repeat. Above all, smile! That always helps.

Communicate a Positive Message

As a cheerleader, you should always keep in mind that the way you act, cheer, talk and look affects the image of your team and school. Because a cheerleader is really a leader, your attitude is one that others will notice. Be sure yours is a positive attitude, whether your team is winning or losing.

The cheers, also, will be an example of your attitude and sportsmanship. Don't stoop to leading yells that make fun of the other team. Show that your sportsmanship is the right kind.

Introduce yourself to the cheerleaders from the other team. Congratulate them if their team wins. Don't "rub it in" if they lose. Show respect for the coaches and the referees. Make your team and its fans proud to have you leading the cheers.

YOU CAN DO IT!

2 Look Like A Winner

Cheerleading is such great exercise! But things such as proper eating, sleeping, and cleanliness also help give you that "healthy glow."

Eat Right

To look good, you've got to feel good. Feeling good starts with good nutrition. If you are not used to eating three complete meals a day, this will be a good time to begin this healthy habit. Eat a well-balanced diet, including foods from the various food groups. At snack time, choose foods that build energy. Snacks such as fruit, sunflower seeds, raisins and roasted nuts are good choices.

Get Plenty of Sleep and Rest

You've heard it all of your life, and now you're hearing it again — don't stay up too late! Sleep is your body's way of refreshing the mind and restoring energy. In other words, it helps keep you going strong. Because your body needs 8 to 10 hours of sleep each night, what time do you need to go to bed? Don't skimp on sleep. It's good for you.

The Clean Look

"Wash your face!" "Brush your teeth!" "Take a bath!" "Comb your hair!" Do any of these sound familiar? You have probably heard them most of your life. Keep them in mind. Cheerleaders must always look their best.

Nails: if you use nail polish, it's best to use a neutral or clear polish when in uniform. Extremely dark or bright nail polishes will stand out and might even clash with your outfit.

Hair: your hair should be kept clean,

brushed and out of your face. Long hair should be kept pulled back. Short hairstyles can also be very comfortable for cheerleading. Sometimes a good hair spray will be useful to keep your hair in place during the games and practices.

Long or short, it is better to keep your hair fixed in such a way that it doesn't need to be brushed during the event.

Poise and Confidence

Think about your favorite cheerleader — the one you most want to be like. What is it about him or her that is different? Probably it is that person's poise and confidence.

Take a good look at yourself in the mirror. Notice the way that you stand, the way you place your hands and the way you hold your head. Do you look like the person you most want to be like? If not, don't be discouraged. Just tell yourself to keep your shoulders back, hold in your stomach and stand up straight. Practice these things often enough, and soon you'll know what poise really means.

And don't forget confidence. A positive attitude shows you are well prepared. (That's different from the know-it-all attitude.) Practice, practice, practice! That will help you feel good about yourself and your abilities, and it will show!

YOU CAN DO IT!

3 Choosing Your Equipment

Choosing your cheerleading equipment is always exciting. Just remember that the choices you make are one's you will have to live with for your cheering season.

Uniforms

Picking out a cheerleading uniform is serious business. While some squads have only one uniform, others may have six different uniforms and two practice sweatsuits. Obviously, the number of uniforms you choose will depend on the amount of money you are able to spend. If you are trying to keep your cost down, think about choosing one uniform that can be worn comfortably in the fall, winter and spring.

You will also want to be sure that the uniform you choose is durable and comfortable. The uniform must be made to withstand all that jumping and hopping. Try it on for size. You will need to be able to move freely for those jumps and kicks.

A uniform that is durable and keeps its shape (even after many washings), one that is comfortable and one that looks good — that's where to spend your money.

Shoes

Good shoes are a vital part of a cheerleader's equipment. Lightweight shoes with plenty of arch support are usually the most comfortable. Proper arch support will help prevent aches and pains in your feet and legs.

When choosing cheerleading shoes, look for those that have a smooth surface underneath. Stay away from shoes with thick tread. They only leave unnecessary marks on the backs and shoulders of your stunt partners. Put yourself in their place. That wouldn't be very comfortable, would it?

Accessories

Along with a uniform and shoes, you will need to choose several accessories to finish the outfit. Keep in mind the amount of money you are able to spend. If the accessory is out of your budget, start saving for next year.

For example, if you have chosen only one uniform to wear for the different seasons of the year, you may want to pick a matching jacket or sweater that can be worn in colder weather. Also, you may choose tights and socks that match your school's colors. Mix and match them to give your one uniform a different look from time to time. Remember colorful hairbows for that finished look!

Jewelry

Everyone enjoys wearing fashionable jewelry, but when in uniform there are a few things to keep in mind. Wear small posted or stud earrings. Anything that hangs could be accidentally yanked out of your ear during a jump or stunt. Avoid wearing necklaces, especially those with charms or ornaments. Remove rings and bracelets; these can be thrown off during cheerleading activities and lost forever on the sidelines. The best advice is: leave all jewelry at home.

Mega What?

Megaphone literally means, "big voice." This definition gives a very clear picture of what the megaphone really does. It makes your voice sound louder. For those times when you are giving directions to fans or when you shout encouragement to the players, you definitely want to be heard. Megaphones come in all sizes and colors. From eight inches to two feet long, megaphones can be decorated with the cheerleader's name or a picture of the team mascot. It's the size of your megaphone that will make a difference in your decoration.

No matter what your megaphone looks like, take care of it and enjoy using it when you need a "big voice."

Pompons

Pompons are another good addition to your cheerleading equipment. And what choices! They can be made of paper or vinyl. They come with wooden handles, plastic handles or no handles. They can be one color or many colors; thick-stranded or thin-stranded; and the strands can be long or short.

Because colored paper will fade in rain, it might be better to choose vinyl pompons.

Pompons add a flair of color to any sideline cheer. Practice using them together. Make up a routine to show your fans. Have fun!

YOU CAN DO IT!

4 Preparatory Stretches

Flexibility is one of your most important assets as a cheerleader. As long as your muscles are loose and flexible, your cheerleading form will be at its peak. Stunts, kicks and jumps will be easier and will look sharper.

To develop the right flexibility will mean stretching each and every time you prepare for a game, practice or contest. Try to stretch a little further each time a particular stretch is repeated. In this way, your flexibility will improve without too many "sore" muscles.

Do These Nine Warm-Up Stretches:

Neck Roll

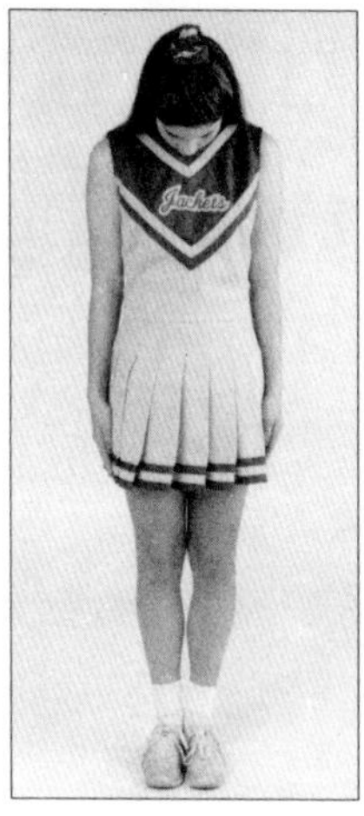

1. Starting in the beginning stance, slowly lower your head forward.
2. Roll your head slowly to the right, until your chin is at the right shoulder.
3. From there, roll your head very slowly back toward the front, and then to your left shoulder. Never completely rotate the head around to the back because this is very harmful to the vertebrae.
4. Repeat three times on each side.
5. Return to beginning stance.

Neck Stretch

1. Turn your head slowly to the right to look over your right shoulder.
2. Again, very slowly, turn your head all the way to the left, looking over the left shoulder.
3. Repeat neck stretch three times on each side.
4. Return to beginning stance.

Shoulder Lifts

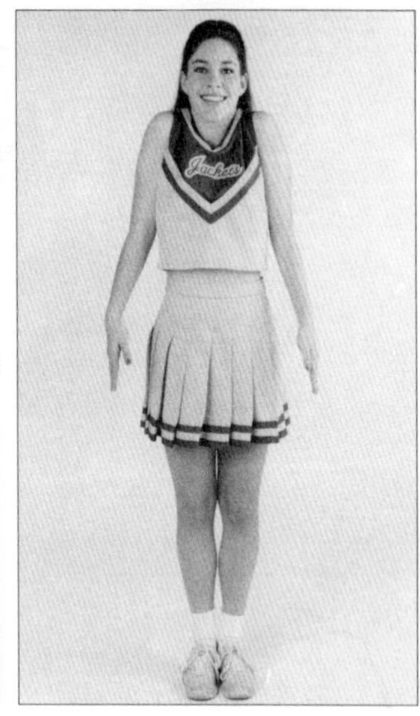

1. Relax your shoulders and slowly lift them up to the ears, then lower.
2. Repeat six times.
3. Return to beginning stance.

Arm Circles

1. Lift your arms straight out to both sides.
2. Move them toward the front in large circular motions.
3. Repeat arm circles to the front several times.
4. Reverse the direction and circle to the back several times.
5. Return to beginning stance.

Pectoral Stretch

1. Clasp your hands behind your hips.
2. Keeping your arms and torso straight, lift your hands until resistance is met.
3. Hold for the count of three, then lower.

Pike Stretch

1. Next, sit down, being careful to keep your back straight.
2. Extend your legs to the front, keeping them straight and close together.
3. Grasp your legs underneath the ankles,

point your toes and pull forward until it hurts a little bit.

4. Hold for the count of three.
5. Repeat.

Straddle Stretch

1. With your back straight, seated in pike position, slowly spread your legs apart as far as possible.

2. With toes pointed, turn your torso toward the right foot. Lift your chin and stretch out over the right leg as if to bring your chest to the right knee. Keep your chin

reaching toward your toes.

3. Grasp your ankle and gently hold for the count of three.

4. Repeat stretch three times on each side.

Split Stretch

1. Sit up straight, remaining in a straddle position. Place your right hand behind your hips, and your left hand in front of your hips. Face the right leg.

3. Slightly lift your body off the ground and lower yourself into a right split. Keep your hands firmly on the ground to prevent

"splitting" more than is comfortable. The top of the left foot should be on the ground with toes pointed. The right foot should be up with your toes also pointed.

4. Hold three counts to increase flexibility.
5. Return to straddle position.
6. Repeat split stretch to the left.
7. Return to beginning stance.

YOU CAN DO IT!

5 Basic Cheerleading Techniques

Soccer players must learn the rules of soccer. Swimmers must learn the butterfly stroke. Football players must learn the various plays and rules of their game. Like every other sport, cheerleading has its own set of rules. These rules are called techniques. Learning cheerleading techniques means understanding the right way to do motions, jumps and stunts.

Because cheerleading is a precision sport, there are many details that must be learned if you want to look sharp while performing. The ability to make clear and precise movements means having "good form." Having good form means that you and your squad make the correct movements at exactly the same moment. This makes your squad work like a finely tuned machine, with all parts working together properly.

Voice Projection

One other important part of good cheerleading techniques is voice projection. You may wonder exactly what that means. It simply means using your voice loudly and strongly, without hurting your vocal chords. We might also say that voice projection is the right way to talk loudly. Be careful not to yell in a high-pitched or shrill, whiny tone. This can harm your vocal chords as well as annoy your audience!

Proper voicing is something that professional singers and actors must learn. You, too, must learn that stronger voicing comes by pushing air through your vocal chords. The air is forced by the flexing of a muscle in your stomach, called the diaphragm. To see if you are using your diaphragm properly, test yourself by lying on your back on the floor. Place a book on your stomach, breathe in deeply, and as you exhale, shout, "Go Bears!" If the book moves when you yell, you are yelling from your diaphragm.

Beginning Stance

Every cheer must start somewhere. That starting place is called the "beginning stance." (Some squads call this "standing at attention.") Before starting a cheer, stand straight with your shoulders, back, face and eyes forward. Your feet should be together, also pointing straight ahead. Your hands should be in blades, fingers together and very straight. Your arms should be hanging straight down at your sides, with the palms of your hands resting on your outer thighs. That's the beginning stance.

Hand Motions

Before we can learn the correct hand motions, there is one common mistake that cheerleaders often make with their hands. They often fail to hold their wrists in a straight or "tight" position. "Broken" wrists can make a cheer look sloppy. "Tight" wrists can make arms look as straight as arrows.

Practice The Following Hand Motions:

Blades

In this position, your hand looks like a blade, with the middle finger being the very tip.

1. Straighten all of your fingers and keep them close together.
2. Slightly cup the palm of your hand to keep your fingers from arching backwards.

Daggers

In this position your hand is supposedly holding a dagger.

1. Make a fist with your hand, with the thumb lying across the second digit of your fingers.
2 Bend your elbow so that the thumb end of the fist is next to your chest.
3. Notice that your fist is now horizontal.

Candlesticks

To remember candlesticks, imagine holding a candlestick straight up so that melting wax won't drip anywhere.

1. Make a fist with your hand, with the thumb lying across the second digit of your fingers.
2. Notice the vertical position of your fist.

Buckets

Think of holding a bucket of water in each hand.

1. Make a fist with your hand like you do in candlesticks.
2. Make sure your wrists are tight.

Clap

This type of clap is used for a precise look in cheers; it won't make a loud sound.

1. Slightly cup your palms together with neither one facing the ground.
2. Bend your fingers and thumbs in over the outside of your hands.

Hands on Hips

Bend elbows and place your fists on your hips.

1. The palms of your hands should face backward.
2. Your elbows should point straight out to the side in opposite directions.
3. Remember to keep your hands fisted and your wrists tight.

Arm Positions

For an arm motion to look sharp and precise, it must have a well-defined beginning and ending place. The following tips help improve your arm movements and make your cheers look sharper.

There are two kinds of arm motions: vertical (up and down) and horizontal (front to side). For vertical motions your elbows should stop at your temples so your arms are covering your ears. When bringing arms up on each side of your body, imagine they are steel rods that cannot be bent. (You don't want "flying arms" that don't know where to start and stop!)

Horizontal arm motions are made from the front to the sides. Imagine that you are standing with your back against the wall. Your arms would not be able to go any farther than the level surface of the wall. That is as far as they should go, no matter where you stand. If you swing your arms too far back, it takes away from that neat look you desire as a precision "cheerleading machine."

High V

This positions your arms to look like a V.

1. If you were the face of a clock, one of your arms would be at 1:30 and the other arm would be at 10:30.
2. Make sure your hands point in the same direction as your arms, continuing the line your arms have started. In other words, don't let your hands droop or flop!

Inverted V or Low V

An Inverted V is an upside-down High V. It goes at a downward angle.

Vertical Arms

Both arms should be straight up and parallel to one another.

1. Keep your palms facing each other.
2. Make sure your arms do not go behind your ears.

Feet and Leg Positions

You might not have thought that there would be specific motions for the legs. But there are a few. When you move your legs, you'll want to do it with purpose. Don't be lazy. Although improper leg movements are not as noticeable as improper arm movements, they can still affect your squad's performance. Some general rules about leg movements are included in this section.

When you are standing still, where do your feet point? For proper cheerleading form, they should be pointing forward. (If you make an effort to stand this way at all times, that will be one less thing for you to think about when you're out there in front of the cheering fans.) When you lift your foot off the ground, point your toes and keep the top of your foot facing the audience.

Some Helpful Hints:

Kicks

There are two common types of kicks:

1. **Low kicks** are sometimes used in cheers. Your "kicking" foot should be lifted to about mid-shin of the other leg.
2. **High kicks** should be kicked as high as possible. They are used in pompon routines, fast chants and in place of a jump to show enthusiasm.

Side Leg Lifts

When you do a side leg lift, you normally will lift your leg to the height of your hip. Remember to keep your toes pointed and the top of your foot facing the audience.

Knee Lifts

As you lift your knee, your pointed foot should slide up the inside of your other leg. The heel of the foot you are lifting should reach the knee of your other leg.

Knee Bends

When you do knee bends, your feet and knees should stay parallel to each other throughout the bend. Be careful not to let your legs spread outward as you bend them. Do knee bends with your feet and legs together.

Lunges

Lunges can be done to the front or to the side. Slightly lift and move one of your legs about 14 inches away from the other, either to the front or to the side. The lifted leg should come down and remain in a bent-

knee position. Your other leg should stay straight.

1. Side lunges can be done to either side. Shift the weight of your body to the bent leg. The foot of the bent leg should be

placed at a slightly forward angle. The other foot should point toward the audience.

2. Front lunges can be done with either leg. Both feet should point forward. Shift your weight to the front leg and make sure the back leg is directly behind you, not angled out.

YOU CAN DO IT!

6
Cheers!

Just what is this thing called a cheer that you are supposed to be leading? A cheer is a shouted statement that is accompanied by arm and leg movements. (Of course, if you go by that definition alone, then your mom would be cheering when she shakes her finger and yells, "I told you to clean up that mess in your room!") Actually, a cheer is a shout of encouragement accompanied by precise arm and leg movements.

Cheers are attention grabbers. Cheers are entertaining. If you are like me, you enjoy watching a talented cheerleading squad that works together to produce an award winning cheer. They strive to do their best. They give cheers at the right times (pregame, halftime, quarter breaks and time-outs).

In this chapter we will show you photographs of real cheerleaders as they perform these four popular cheers: C'Mon Crowd, Up and Down, Get Up On Your Feet, Shoot The Hoop and When We Say. Study the words for each cheer and then turn the pages and follow along as you look at the photographs.

As you learn these words and motions, you will be able to turn them into something that will fire up your audience.

C'mon Crowd

C'mon Crowd is great for pep rallies and games. Encourage the fans to shout along as you yell out your team name or school initials. Pompons can be used to accentuate words, and this cheer can be done in rounds (one after the other) if you have at least four cheerleaders.

C'MON (clap) CROWD (clap)
YELL IT LOUD! (clap)(clap)
GIVE US AN A! (clap) (A!)
GIVE US AN H! (clap) (H!)
GIVE US AN S! (clap) (S!)
PUT IT ALL TOGETHER
A - H - S!

Up and Down

This cheer combines precision with a little boogie to make a fun cheer for any sporting event.

(slap thighs)
UP (pause) AND DOWN (slap thighs)
OUR TEAM DON'T MESS A-ROUND
CAUSE WE ARE THE BEST
FROM THE EAST TO THE WEST
AND WHEN OUR TEAM IS UP
YOU'RE DOWN!

Get Up On Your Feet

This is a great cheer for pep rallies. The jump incorporated at the end emphasizes the words.

GET UP ON YOUR FEET
AND YELL 3 GO'S!
GO! GO! GO!

GET UP ON YOUR FEET
AND YELL 3 FIGHTS!
FIGHT! FIGHT! FIGHT!

GET UP ON YOUR FEET
AND YELL 3 WINS!
WIN! WIN! WIN!

GET UP ON YOUR FEET
AND YELL GO! FIGHT! WIN!
GO! FIGHT! WIN!

Shoot The Hoop

This cheer is great for breaks during basketball games.

(pause) SHOOT (clap) THE HOOP (slap thighs)
DROP IT THROUGH THE LOOP
OVER THE RIM
TWO POINTS WILL HELP US WIN
TWO POINTS (clap) (clap) (clap)
TWO POINTS (clap) (clap) (clap)
TWO POINTS (clap) (clap) (clap)
SHOOT TWO!

When We Say

This cheer is an oldie, but goodie. Wipe the dust off this cheer, and use it to push your team on for a victory. For variety, use this cheer with pompons.

WHEN WE SAY BLUE
SAY LET'S GO!
BLUE! (LET'S GO!)
BLUE! (LET'S GO!)

WHEN WE SAY HEIGHTS
SAY LET'S FIGHT!
HEIGHTS! (LET'S FIGHT!)
HEIGHTS! (LET'S FIGHT!)

WHEN WE SAY WIN
SAY TONIGHT!
WIN! (TONIGHT!)
WIN! (TONIGHT!)

GO FIGHT WIN!
LET'S YELL IT!
GO FIGHT WIN!

Turn the page to see the motions for each of these cheers.

C'Mon Crowd

C'MON (clap) CROWD (clap)

YELL IT LOUD (clap) (clap)

GIVE US AN A! (clap) (A!)

GIVE US AN H! (clap) (H!)

GIVE US AN S! (clap) (S!)

PUT IT/ALL/TOGETHER A! H! S!

Up and Down

(pause)
UP
(pause)
AND DOWN
(slap)
OUR TEAM
DON'T MESS
AROUND
(clap)
CAUSE
WE ARE
THE BEST

FROM THE | EAST TO | THE WEST | AND

WHEN | OUR | TEAM | IS

UP | pause) | YOU'RE | DOWN!

Get Up On Your Feet

GET UP  ON YOUR  FEET

AND YELL  THREE  GO'S!

GO! GO! GO!

Repeat motions at left for verse two. Then do last verse:

GET UP

ON YOUR

FEET

AND YELL

GO!

FIGHT!

WIN!

Repeat
GO!
FIGHT!
WIN!

Shoot The Hoop

(slap) SHOOT (clap) THE HOOP

(Slap) DROP IT THROUGH THE LOOP

(clap) OVER (pause) THE RIM

(slap)
TWO POINTS WILL HELP
US WIN
TWO
POINTS
(clap)
(clap)
(clap)
TWO
POINTS
(clap)
(clap)
(clap)

(next page)

Shoot The Hoop (continued)

TWO POINTS (clap) (clap) (clap)

SHOOT TWO!

When We Say

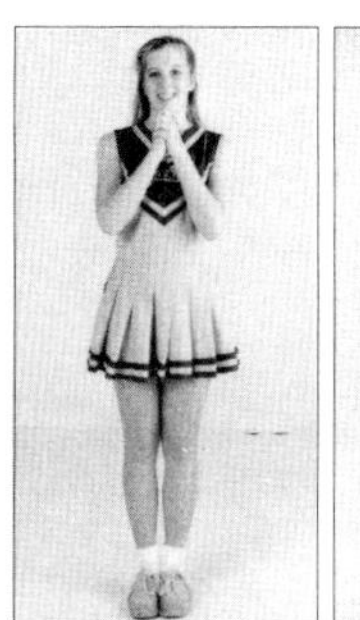
WHEN WE

SAY BLUE

SAY

LET'S GO!

BLUE!

LET'S GO!

BLUE!

(LET'S GO!)

WHEN WE

SAY HEIGHTS

SAY

LET'S FIGHT!

(next page)

When We Say (continued)

HEIGHTS!

(LET'S FIGHT!)

HEIGHTS!

(LET'S FIGHT!)

WHEN WE

SAY WIN!

SAY

TONIGHT!

WIN!

(TONIGHT!)

WIN!

(TONIGHT!)

GO!

FIGHT!

WIN!

LET'S YELL IT!

GO!

FIGHT!

WIN!

Choose from the hand, arm and leg motions that you have learned and apply them to the next four cheers.

Go Team

Pick up your pompons and divide your squad into three groups to do this cheer in rounds. While each group's members do their section, the other groups stand still and yell. Don't forget to smile!

Group 1:
GO TEAM (clap) (clap)
GO TEAM (clap) (clap)
GO T-E-A-M TEAM (clap) (clap)

Group 2:
FIGHT TEAM (clap) (clap)
FIGHT TEAM (clap) (clap)
FIGHT T-E-A-M TEAM (clap) (clap)

Group 3:
WIN TEAM (clap) (clap)
WIN TEAM (clap) (clap)
WIN T-E-A-M TEAM (clap) (clap)

Group 1:
GO!

Group 2:
FIGHT!

Group 3:
WIN!

Hey, Gang

This is a really fun cheer that encourages crowd response. Use it as often as you can and substitute the names of school mascots, including your own.

HEY, GANG
WILL THE RAIDERS WIN THIS GAME TONIGHT?
WELL, NO!
THEN WHO WILL WIN IT?
YELL IT, SPELL IT
B-B-BRO
(clap 5 times, echoing cadence of letters shouted)
N-N-COS
(repeat clap cadence, as above)
B-R-O (clap) (clap) (clap)
N-C-O-S (clap) (clap) (clap)
BRONCOS! BRONCOS! BRONCOS!

Who Are

Another cheer that encourages the crowd to respond to its many questions. Punctuate the end of this cheer with a spread eagle or tuck jump.

WHO ARE
THE RAIDERS?
WE ARE
THE RAIDERS!
WHAT KIND

OF RAIDERS?
FIGHTING RAIDERS!
WELL, STAND UP
YOU RAIDERS
AND YELL!

F-I-G-H-T

The slow, methodic rhythm of this cheer allows plenty of time to build complicated pyramids.

F I-G-H-T
F **I** G-H-T
F-I **G** H-T
F-I-G **H** T
F-I-G-H **T**
F - I - G - H - T!

YOU CAN DO IT!

7 Chants

Performing chants can be thrilling. They are naturally rhythmic and repetitive sayings, often without motions. Unlike cheers, which must be performed very "machine like," chants allow for more individuality. Dance steps, pompon claps, kicks, bounces and lots of energy can be added to make your own chant routines. Even clapping or stomping to the rhythm of the chant will add some pizzazz.

The following chants are divided into several groups to give you an idea of when to use them. Offensive chants are used to encourage your team to score, and defensive chants are useful when the other team has the ball (such as during the last few seconds of a close basketball game or when your football team is at the goal line and about to score).

Offensive Football Chant

ALL THE WAY
DOWN THE FIELD [COURT]
DON'T (clap) STOP!

Offensive Football Chant

SCORE SIX POINTS
TAKE IT DOWN TO THAT GOAL
S-I-X SCORE SIX

Offensive Football Chant

WE'RE RUNNIN' FOR A TOUCHDOWN
WE'RE MOVIN' T'WARD THE GOAL
WE ARE THE PANTHERS
AND WE ARE IN CONTROL!

Offensive Basketball Chant

SET IT UP. (clap)(clap)
PUT IT IN. (clap)(clap)
SET IT UP, PUT IT IN,
LET'S WIN!

Offensive Basketball Chant

DRIBBLE IT. (clap)(clap)
PASS IT. (clap)(clap)
DRIBBLE IT, PASS IT,
WE WANT A BASKET!

Offensive Basketball Chant

REEE-BOUND, LONGHORNS,
REEE-BOUND (clap)

Offensive Basketball Chant

SHOOT 2, 2
SHOOT 2, 2
SHOOT 2, 2
SHOOT 2!

Offensive Basketball Chant

R-E
R-E-B
R-E-B-O-U-N-D
REBOUND!

Defensive Chant

HEY!
HEY, HEY!
HEY, HEY!
TAKE IT AWAY!

Defensive Chant

HEY, HEY, HEY, HEY (echo)
TAKE THAT BALL AWAY! (echo)

Defensive Football Chant

ELIMINATE THE END. (clap)
ELIMINATE THE BACK. (clap)(clap)
WE'VE GOT THE DEFENSE.
THEY'VE GOT THE BALL.
(stomp)(clap)(stomp)(clap)
ATTACK!

Defensive Chant

THEY'VE GOT THE BALL,
THEY'VE GOT THE BALL, TROJANS
THEY'VE GOT THE BALL,
WE WANT THE BALL TROJANS, GO!
(clap)(clap) TROJANS, GO!

Defensive Chant

GET THAT BALL,
GET THAT BALL,
GET THAT BALL AND GO! HEY!

Crowd Rouser

S-P (echo)
I-R (echo)
I-T (echo)
GOT SPIRIT? UH-HUH!
WELL LET'S HEAR IT! OKAY!
(Raise volume with each repetition of this chant.)

Crowd Rouser

WE'RE CRAZY, THAT'S WHAT I SAID
WE'RE CRAZY, WE'RE GONNA KNOCK 'EM DEAD
WE'RE C-R-A-Z-Y. ARE WE SO CRAZY?

Crowd Rouser

S-P-IR-IT, SPIRIT, LET'S HEAR IT!

Crowd Rouser

WHEN WE SAY, "GO," YOU SAY, "RAIDERS".
GO (RAIDERS)
GO (RAIDERS)
WHEN WE SAY, "FIGHT," YOU SAY, "RAIDERS".
FIGHT (RAIDERS)
FIGHT (RAIDERS)
WHEN WE SAY, "WIN," YOU SAY, "RAIDERS".
WIN (RAIDERS)
WIN (RAIDERS)
WHEN WE SAY, "BEAT," YOU SAY, "TIGERS".
BEAT (TIGERS)
BEAT (TIGERS)!

Crowd Rouser

LET'S GET A LITTLE BIT ROWDY
R-O-W (clap)(clap) uh D-Y!

Crowd Rouser

WE'RE ROWDY, WE'RE ROUGH.
WE'RE BIG AND MEAN AND TOUGH.
WE'RE ROWDY, ROUGH, MEAN AND TOUGH.
I SAY, WE'RE ROUGH AND TOUGH!

Crowd Rouser

(loudly) V-I-C-T-O-R-Y, V-I-C-T-O-R-Y!
(softly) V-I-C-T-O-R-Y, V-I-C-T-O-R-Y!

Crowd Rouser

WE'RE BUSTIN' LOOSE.
WE'RE GONNA COOK YOUR GOOSE.
THE COWBOY TEAM IS ON THE ROMP.
(repeat)
WE ARE THE (stomp as you say:)
C (clap) (stomp, stomp, stomp) (clap)
O (clap) (stomp, stomp, stomp) (clap)
W (clap) (stomp, stomp, stomp) (clap)
B (clap) (stomp, stomp, stomp) (clap)
O (clap) (stomp, stomp, stomp) (clap)
Y (clap) (stomp, stomp, stomp) (clap)
S (clap) (stomp, stomp, stomp) (clap)
(stomp once as you say:)
COWBOYS! (clap)
(then stomp with each word as you say:)
WE ARE THE BEST!

Crowd Rouser

TAKE IT TO THE LIMIT. (echo)
TAKE IT TO THE MAX. (echo)
WE, THE MIGHTY BRONCOS, (echo)
WILL SHOW YOU WHERE IT'S AT. (echo)

Crowd Rouser

(quietly) BOOM, SHA BOOM,
SHA BOOM, BOOM, BOOM
(Repeat phrase a little louder.)
(Repeat a third time, end with a loud BOOM!)

Crowd Rouser

TAKE IT TO THE TOP, HEY!
THE RAIDER TEAM IS GONNA WIN IT.
THE RAIDER TEAM IS RUNNIN' HOT.
SO LET'S TAKE IT
TO THE LIMIT!

Footloose

Spice up your chants with some fancy footwork. To run in place cheerleader-style, keep your legs together and bounce from one foot to the other, alternately pointing the toe and planting your foot on the ground. The pointed toe should touch the ground right next to the big toe of the foot that is flat on the ground. To stay in the same place, remember to shift your weight from side to side, keeping your weight on the foot that is on the ground.

YOU CAN DO IT!

8

Jumps

Jumps are used in cheerleading to show enthusiasm and energy. Cheerleaders commonly do a jump at the end of cheers and chants for a spirited finale. I like to think of jumps as human exclamation points! By following these tips, your jump form can improve dramatically. Remember, the higher the jump, the better!

Keep your toes pointed from the start to the finish.

Keep your back straight, your shoulders level, and your eyes forward.

Never look down because this will make you jump lower. Bring your legs up to your arms instead of reaching down to your feet. This makes the jump look higher, and it keeps your back straight.

Finish every jump with your legs together and your feet in a parallel position.

Try These Jumps

The Banana

This simple jump can be done alone or used as a pre-jump to build momentum for a more difficult jump.

1. Begin with your arms straight down at your sides, your hands in blades and your feet in parallel position.
2. Slightly bend your knees, preparing for a lift-off.
3. Keep your arms parallel to one another throughout the entire jump. Beginning with your arms at your sides, swing forward until your upper arms are alongside your ears.
4. As your arms swing forward, your back arches and your legs swing back to form the shape of a banana.

The Tuck

This jump is simple to do, but perfect for incorporating into cheers.

1. With your feet in parallel position and keeping legs together, bring your knees up to your chest to "tuck" into a ball.

2. Wrap your arms tightly around both shins, as if hugging your legs, at the climax of the jump.
3. As your feet are returning to the ground, raise your arms in High V or Salute to give this simple jump a great ending.

The Spread Eagle

Try this jump alone or as a pre-jump to the Straddle.

1. Arms straight down, hands in blades and feet in parallel position.
2. Bend your knees slightly to push off the

ground.

3. Swing your arms forward, raising them into a High V. Your palms will face out at the climax of the jump.
4. As your arms swing up, spread your legs into an inverted V.

The Herkie

This jump was invented by H.L. Herkimer, the founder of the National Cheerleaders Association. It has many variations in form.

1. In mid-air, one leg will point straight out to the side and the other will be bent.

a. One variation of this jump has the bent knee pointing to the ground with the toes pointing up.

b. Another variation is for the bent knee to face the audience with the toes pointing to the background (with the goal of forming a line from the pointed toe of the straight leg to the knee of the bent leg).

2. The beauty of this jump is its many variations! Choose a favorite arm position or experiment with all of these variations.

a. Place one arm on your hip while saluting with the other.

b. Place both arms on your hips, keeping both hands fisted.

c. With your hands in blades, extend one hand toward the extended foot while bending your other arm. The bent elbow should be directly above and parallel to the bent knee.

The Straddle

This is a difficult jump, but very effective if performed correctly. It is generally necessary to do a pre-jump with the Straddle in order to gain momentum and height.

1. Straight legs should be lifted and extended out to the sides as far as possible in the straddle position.
2. With your hands in blades, extend your arms and hands toward your toes (hence the nickname, "Toe-toucher").
3. Your arms can also extend straight out in front with hands clasped.

The Pike

This is another difficult, but beautiful jump. It should be performed with one side toward the audience. A Banana pre-jump works very well with this jump.

1. With your legs together and straight, lift them forward, horizontal with the hips.
2. Extend your arms out toward your toes, keeping them parallel to your legs. Your hands should be in blades.

YOU CAN DO IT!

9 Simple Stunts

Good stunts add a daring element to your cheerleading style. Stunts can be included in your cheers in much the same way as jumps. They also add creativity to sideline chants and pompon routines. Some cheerleading squads use stunts to begin every football game. They do shoulder mounts during every kick-off. From atop their partners' shoulders, members do chants and motions until the opening play is over.

An experienced cheerleader can make a difficult stunt look very simple. Although stunts described in this chapter are not difficult, be careful to practice them with an adult spotter at all times.

There are a few basic steps to follow when putting a stunt into a cheer. First, measure how many beats (counts) it takes for your squad to "build" a stunt. Don't forget to add a count for the ending pose. Next, subtract the number of beats from the end of the cheer (beats include syllables, pauses and claps). This identifies the place you will need to begin the stunt in that cheer.

Partner Stunts

Partner stunts are done by two people. The person on the bottom of the stunt is called the "base." This should be the heavier or stronger of the partners. The base should always keep her legs at least shoulder width apart to provide a sturdy foundation.

Mount refers to the person doing the climbing. The mount will usually be the smaller or less heavy of the two. The mount and base should always signal one another before climbing or dismounting from a stunt.

The signal could be a verbal "okay" or a non-verbal hand squeeze. Both partners should agree on the signal before performing the stunt. If either partner starts to have trouble, he or she should yell "down" and everyone should dismount immediately.

Some of these partner stunts are very simple and others are not. Please do not attempt these partner stunts without an adult spotter.

The Pony Mount
(Four counts to build)

1. Base — with your legs and feet in beginning position, slightly bend down and place your open palms right above your knees. Your fingers should be together, with your thumb spread to the other side of your knee. Distribute your weight toward your knees and feet. Slightly arch your back, being careful not to lunge forward.
2. Mount — while standing directly behind base, place both hands in the small of her back, one hand slightly above the other.

The Pony Mount

3. Mount — using the base as support, gently lift off the ground and:

   a. for a Seated Pony Mount, straddle the waist of the base. (Do not run and jump on the base; this could push the base forward.) At the same time, pull bent knees in tight point, toes toward back, and "hug" the waist of the base with your thighs.

   b. for a Standing Pony Mount, place your knees on the hips of the base. Next, carefully place one foot at a time on the small of the base's back. Make sure you have

your balance as you stand up.

4. Complete the Pony Mount with any of the following variations:

   a. The mount can raise arms to High V, horizontal or any choice of arm positions.

   b. If the base and mount are properly positioned, they can simultaneously extend arms horizontally for a dynamic ending.

   c. This stunt can be performed, very carefully, with the mount holding pompons.

5. Mount — dismount by returning hands to small of back and lifting off.

The Shoulder Mount

The Shoulder Mount
(Four to five counts to build)

1. Base — bend your right knee, sliding the left leg straight to the left side.
   Mount — step up slightly behind and to the right of the base.
2. Mount — place your right foot in the right hip socket of the base.
   Base — grasp the right knee of the mount with your right hand. Your right shoulder moves behind the right knee of the mount.
3. Mount — swing your left leg up and over the left shoulder of the base, and rest

bottom on the shoulders of the base. Distribute your weight evenly over both shoulders of the base. Tuck your feet behind the base's ribs.

4. Variations on Shoulder Mount:

   a. The mount can choose any arm motion to end a cheer.

   b. Both the base and mount can extend arms horizontally.

   c. Yell an entire chant from this position.

5. Dismount:

   a. Base — swing your arms down from behind the mount's legs to in front of the

mount's thighs, grabbing her hands beside your neck.

b. Mount — grab the hands of the base, and squeeze to signal dismount.

c. Base — thrust your shoulders back.

d. Mount — pop your legs off the base's shoulders and into a straddle before quickly bringing them together to land. (In this way, the mount lands directly behind the base, with her hands on the base's shoulders.)

The "L" Stand

(Three to five count to build)

1. Base — perform a side lunge, with the foot of your bent leg pointing to the side for more stability.

   Mount — step up slightly behind the bent leg of the base.
2. Mount — place your foot in the hip socket of the base (right on right, left on left).

   Base — grasp the Mount around the knee as she places her foot in your hip socket. Your shoulder will move behind her knee.
3. Mount — extend your free leg horizontally above the base's head as you straighten the leg that is secured at the base's hip.

   Base — extend your free arm at an angle to grab the mount's extended leg at the ankle. Your thumb should be in front of the ankle with your fingers wrapped behind the ankle.
4. Mount — extend one arm horizontally to correspond with the horizontal leg. Extend your other arm vertically.
5. Dismount in the exact opposite order that you mounted.

PARTNER STUNT COMBINATIONS

Two "L's" and a Pony

(Three to five counts to build)

Simultaneously build two L stands with a Pony Stand in the middle for a winning combination.

Two Ponies and a Shoulder Mount

(Three to five counts to build)

Put a Shoulder Mount between two Pony Mounts, and then extend your arms vertically for a sharp ending for this stunt.

GROUP STUNTS

(At least six people)

The Split Lift

(Six to eight counts to build)

1. Following guidelines 1-3, form two Shoulder Mounts, one (Shoulder Mount A) standing directly in front of the other (Shoulder Mount B). Cheerleaders C and D will then stand at arms length of the Base of Shoulder Mount B, one cheerleader on each side.

2. Shoulder Mount A - both the base and mount should place fisted hands on their hips.
3. Shoulder Mount B
   a. Mount places both hands on mount A's shoulders.
   b. Mount extends legs to either side.
4. Cheerleaders C and D
   a. With elbows bent and pointing down, hands are palm side up and resting on own shoulders.
   b. As mount B extends legs, they should land in both hands of each cheerleader.
   c. Secure legs in palms of hands, with thumbs on one side of legs, fingers toward back of legs.
   d. Simultaneously push arms straight above head, raising mount B into Split Lift to complete an excellent stunt.
5. Dismount
   a. Cheerleaders C and D slowly lower mount B back to shoulders of the Base.
   b. Shoulder mounts A and B dismount according to previous guidelines.

The Pyramid
(Six to eight counts to build)

1. Cheerleaders A, B, and C get on hands and knees.
   a. Arms and legs should be parallel and shoulder-width apart.
   b. Fingers should be together and pointing to audience.
2. Cheerleaders D and E climb onto cheerleaders A,B and C, assuming the same positions.
   a. Cheerleader D will have right hand and leg on cheerleader B, with left hand and leg on cheerleader A.
   b. Cheerleader E places right hand and leg on cheerleader C, with left hand and leg on cheerleader B.
3. Cheerleader F stands on hips of cheerleader B to climb on backs of cheerleaders D and E.
   a. Cheerleader F places right hand and leg on cheerleader E.
   b. Cheerleader F places left hand and leg on cheerleader D.

4. For a dramatic ending to this simple Pyramid, all six cheerleaders should emphasize the last syllable of the cheer with great enthusiasm.
5. Dismount carefully, beginning with cheerleader F, and ending with cheerleaders A,B and C.

YOU CAN DO IT!

10 How to Plan and Lead a Pep Rally

Pep rallies are fun! Having a pep rally is like having a big "cheerleader party" where you get to do all the things you enjoy doing. By planning ahead and adding in a little hard work, you can host a very successful pep rally. A successful pep rally is one that builds the team's spirit and increases team support among the fans. So enlist your artist friends to help make signs and encourage the musicians to prepare a festive song. Getting everyone involved will lead to an enthusiastic pep rally.

Get Organized

You will need to start by getting organized. At least a week in advance, set a date, pick a time and choose a place. Most pep rallies are held in school gyms, but if you don't have one available, don't let that stop you. Small scale pep rallies, called yell-ins, can be held in the school cafeteria, in your front yard or in a parking lot. Once you've chosen a place, date and time, you will need to get permission to hold your pep rally. Pep rallies are usually supervised by adults who are involved with the team. Let them help you with these initial plans. When all systems are go, move ahead by spreading the word.

Let people know about the pep rally by putting up signs that announce the date, time and place. See if announcements can be made at school. Invite all of the team members and their families to come. Encourage everyone to be there. The more, the merrier!

Lastly, you will want to prepare a pep rally schedule. List the planned events and the order in which you want them to take place.

If you want the pep rally to start with a drum cadence, write that down. If you think Coach Jellyroll would give a good pep talk, write it down. Choose the cheers you want to do and schedule them into the pep rally. Once your pep rally schedule is written, it's time to get busy!

Mighty Eagles Pep Rally Schedule

Date: October 12

Time: 2 pm

Place: school gym

Opponent: Tigers

1. Drum Cadence: drummers (players run through sign)
2. Welcome Speech: principal
3. School Fight Song: band (cheerleaders do pompon routine)
4. Cheer: "Victory, Victory"
5. Skit: "Cage the Tigers" (Jimmy, Carol, Beth and Lauren)
6. Chant competition to see which class is most spirited
7. Cheer: "Rise Up to Victory"
8. Cheer: "F-I-G-H-T" (end with split pyramid)
9. Chant: "Spirit, Let's Hear It!"
10. Player of the Week announced: vice-principal
11. Pep Talk: Coach Jellyroll
12. Cheer: "Color Shout" (with pompons)
13. Award Spirit Stick to most spirited class
14. Alma Mater: band (hold up pompons)
15. Dismiss by classes

Get Busy

With your pep rally schedule complete, it's time to get busy. The schedule can now be used as a "to do" list. First, you will need to contact everyone who will have a responsibility in the pep rally. Ask if they are willing to participate. If they are willing, give them a copy of the schedule so they will know exactly what to expect. People are happier to help if they know what is expected of them.

Next, you will need to get busy painting signs. You may want to enlist an art class to help you with this project. Using tempera paint and large rolls of paper, make enough signs to fill the gymnasium walls. Very wide, felt-tipped paint brushes with ink buckets are also available for sign painting, but these are generally more expensive than tempera paint. Either choice will lead to great pep rally signs.

Now turn your creativity button on "high" and start painting. Make one exceptionally long sign for the players to run through. Write something on it like "Break Through For A Victory!" Paint smaller, individual signs for each player. These should have encouraging statements such as "Doing Fine #9" or "You're the Best, Wes!" Make comical signs such as a picture of a kitty cat with the slogan, "Tame the Tigers!" After you've made plenty of signs, roll them back up and store them until pep rally day.

The day before the pep rally is a good time for the cheerleaders to practice the pep rally. Each cheerleader should be assigned a place to stand. Practice every cheer and chant at least two times. Give everyone a copy of the pep rally schedule. Practice the pompon routine. If you have more than one uniform, this is a good time to decide which one you will wear for the pep rally. At this point, everything should be in place for a powerful pep rally.

On pep rally day you can sense the excitement in the air. Arrive in plenty of time to have all the signs hung at least an hour before the rally begins. Use wide masking tape to keep the signs attached securely to the wall. Make sure all of the cheerleaders have their pompons in front of their assigned place, so they can quickly grab them when necessary. Reserve front-row seats for those participating in the rally so they can easily get to the microphone. Having confidence that all preparations have been completed, you are now ready to lead your first pep rally.

Get After It!

Enthusiasm and school spirit are high as the crowd fills the gymnasium. You feel almost electric with excitement. It's a good thing because you will need lots of energy to lead a pep rally. If you start to feel nervous because of the big crowd, pick out a friend in the audience and look at her for a moment. This will make the crowd seem more friendly! Consider everything you've learned about poise, confidence and good cheerleading form; now is the time to put it into action!

Try to keep the pep rally flowing along quickly and actively. Keep something going at all times. If the people doing the skit are taking too much time to get ready, start a quick chant while they get into place. Do plenty of jumps and gymnastics in between each event. Show respect for others involved in the pep rally by standing still while they give their speeches or announcements. If you make a mistake during a cheer or fall down from a stunt, do your best to get back on track as soon as possible. Don't worry about it and don't react by making a terrible face. The audience may not have noticed your mistake, but they will notice your reaction! Have fun with your pep rally. When it's all over, you and your team will be glad you took the effort to do it!

Glossary

Banana — A cheerleading jump in which the backward arch of the arms, back and legs resembles a banana.

Base — Refers to the bottom person(s) of a partner or group stunt.

Beginning Stance — The proper way to begin cheers and chants to ensure continuity of a cheerleading squad.

Blades — Hand position in which all fingers and thumb are together and extended.

Buckets — Hand position in which both arms

are extended horizontally and both hands are fisted, as if holding buckets of water.

Candlesticks — Vertically-fisted hand position.

Cheer — Used in the noun form to denote a shout of declaration or encouragement accompanied by precise arm and leg motions.

Daggers — Horizontally-fisted hand position performed with bent elbows.

Diaphragm — A section of muscle that separates the chest from the abdomen and aids respiration.

Dismount — The proper way to climb down from a partner or group stunt.

Flexibility — In this case, referring to the ability of muscles to be flexed and stretched through their full range of motion without causing undue stress to muscles.

Herkie — A cheerleading jump executed with one leg straight and the other leg bent.

High V — An arm motion in which both arms are extended upward resembling the letter V.

Horizontal — Movements and positions that go across the line of the body, in contrast to up-and-down (vertical) moves.

Inverted V — Denoting an arm or leg position in which the downward angle of the arm/leg resembles an upside-down V (also referred to as Low V).

Lunge — A leg position in which one leg is straight, one leg is bent and both feet are flat on the ground.

Megaphone — Funnel-shaped piece of cheerleading equipment that magnifies the voice. It literally means, "big voice or sound."

Mount — Used in the verb form to denote the proper way to climb onto a partner or group stunt. In the noun form, the word describes the person(s) who climb(s) in a stunt.

Parallel — Two or more lines that never meet, but run alongside each other.

Partner Stunt — A stunt involving two people.

Pectorals — Chest muscles.

Pep Rally — An event organized to encourage athletes and to build team spirit among the fans.

Pike — A stretch or jump executed with arms and legs extended together horizontally.

Pompons — You know, those fluffy things cheerleaders shake. The only tricky thing about this word is how it's spelled.

Pony Mount — A partner stunt in which one person is seated or standing on the other's back.

Precision — Referring to motions that are formed distinctly and correctly.

Pyramid — A group stunt with several people stacked on top of each other, resulting in a triangular form.

Salute — An arm motion in which the arm is bent in toward the head and then extended upward at an angle.

Shoulder Mount— A partner stunt executed with one person sitting on another's shoulders.

Sideline Chant — A repetitive, rhythmic declaration performed with or without motions.

Split — A stretch or stunt executed with both legs extended in opposite directions.

Split Lift — A group stunt focused on a cheerleader lifted high in the split position.

Spread Eagle — A cheerleading jump executed with arms in High V position and legs extended in an Inverted V.

Spotter — A person designated to closely observe stunt formation with the purpose of preventing injury to the people performing the stunt.

Straddle — A jump or stretch executed with the legs wide apart.

Squad — A group or team of cheerleaders.

Tuck — A jump executed with knees bent and pulled up to chest, and arms tightly wrapped around legs.

Vertical — Up-and-down movements and positions.

Voice Projection — Projecting the voice in such a way that the muscles of the diaphragm push the air through the vocal cords, resulting in loud volume without undue stress on vocal cords.

Yell-In — A small-scale pep rally

Resources

The All New Official Cheerleaders Handbook

Neil, Randall and Elaine Hart

New York: Simon & Schuster, Incorporated

Revised 1986.

The Cheerleader Supply Company

2010 Merritt

Garland, Texas 75041

Mailing Address:

P.O. Box 660359

Dallas, Texas 75266

(214) 231-6364

The National Cheerleader's Association (NCA)

2010 Merritt

Garland, Texas 75041

Mailing Address:

P.O. Box 660359

Dallas, Texas 75266

(214) 840-2307